THREE ESSAYS ON MARX'S VALUE THEORY

THREE ESSAYS *on* MARX'S VALUE THEORY

by SAMIR AMIN

MONTHLY REVIEW PRESS

New York

Library of Congress Cataloging-in-Publication Data

Amin, Samir.
  Three essays on Marx's value theory / by Samir Amin.
     pages cm
  Includes bibliographical references.
  ISBN 978-1-58367-424-6 (cloth : alk. paper) 1. Labor theory of value. 2.
Surplus value. 3. Value. 4. Marxian economics. I. Title. II. Title: 3
essays on Marx's value theory.
  HB206.A45 2013
  335.4'12—dc23

                    2013031467

Monthly Review Press
146 West 29th Street, Suite 6W
New York, New York 10001

www.monthlyreview.org

5 4 3 2 1

Contents

1. Social Value and the Price-Income System

I BEGIN WITH A PERSONAL NOTE. I first read Marx when I was twenty years of age and then reread him every twenty years at moments that corresponded to major changes in the course of history. I read him in 1950, when hidden behind the East-West conflict and the first Southern awakening was taking shape, revealed in the 1955 Bandung Conference. In 1970, as director of the African Institute for Economic Development and Planning (IDEP) in Dakar, I formed the project of making Marx a focus for training and discussion that would contribute to radicalization of the way forward opened by the African and Asian peoples' reconquests of their independences. In 1990 the problem Marx could give guidance to was to know what could be salvaged from the shipwreck of the twentieth century's historic socialism. In 2010, with the implosion of the capitalist system that had declared itself the "end of history," Marx's work opened possibilities for new ways forward whose outcomes are yet to be discovered. My readings at each of those moments were directed by my concern to respond to the current challenge. And every time I discovered that Marx was coming to our aid with incomparable power, though obviously on the condition of extending the radical social critique he had begun, rather than to be content with exegesis of his texts.

Smith and Ricardo had founded the new political economy upon their discovery of the law of labor value. As thinkers of the rising bourgeoisie, nourished by the Enlightenment and its praise of reason, they found it natural to put labor at the center of the challenge whose meaning they proposed to decipher. Without, for all that, refusing recognition to the merit of the entrepreneurs whose charge it was to organize efficacious labor processes and whose profit was their legitimate compensation.

Marx, contrary to what has often been said, did not endorse this "law of value," even in a better formulated form. His was a more ambitious project: he aimed to found a radical critique of society in general, starting from a critique of the capitalism then building. He discovered that the concept of social value lay at the heart of his project. In any case that is what results from my reading of Marx, which gives high importance to anthropology. In this reading, labor is unique to the human species and is central to the construction of society. Labor as such, and the social value that it produces, are thus transhistoric concepts. Nevertheless, in the successive stages of history the forms of organization of labor display themselves in particular modes of dress. Seeking to understand these forms, Marx discovered different instances of social organization and how each is specifically articulated with each stage of history. The specific instance for the capitalist stage is economic, which becomes dominant over all others. The critique of capitalism is thus the critique of that dominance—by definition an "anti-economism"—whose efficacy is revealed through the reign of economic/mercantile alienation. The concept of social value allows us to discover the historicity of capitalism.

Marx's critique of classical bourgeois political economy (Smith and Ricardo) started from the requirement that, of necessity, the center of gravity of the analysis be shifted from phenomenal appearances (the observed system of prices and incomes; the "market" and the waves agitating the surface of the sea) to the depths of production governed by the law of value and the extraction of surplus-value, which is capitalism's distinctive form for the extraction of surplus labor. Without this shift of analysis from the phenomenal to the essential, from appearances to the hidden reality, no radical critique of capitalism is possible.

From whatever angle we examine society, especially and obviously from the economic angle, human labor is central to all thought. There is no society, whether ancient, contemporary, or future, in which it is possible to abstract from this basic reality. It is this that defines the human being, both as an individual and as a social being. But the particular conditions through which labor shows itself define the particular nature of every society. Marx's intelligence is shown not in understanding this—others had seen this before him—but in his rigorous analysis of those conditions, starting from the capitalism then being formed and then going back in time, reading what they had been in the past (it is human anatomy that allows us to understand—to read—simian anatomy). It was not by chance that the eighteenth century's *Encyclopedia* was the great book of labor—the labor of farmers, of artisans, of the constructors of canals, wells, fortresses, and palaces—described with precision in all its domains. The rising bourgeoisie, despite the limitations of its project for a new class society, could not, in the elaboration of its social thought, fail to understand the central place of labor. I say "social thought" rather than "social science" in order to avoid the trap into which empiricist positivism fell by confusing social and natural sciences.

Once more let me reiterate: at all stages of human history and whatever the social power relations conditioning its workings, labor is inseparable from the scientific and technological knowledge proper to the period and from the natural (ecological) circumstances in which it takes place. To treat these inseparable dimensions as separate is to act like the theologians for whom body and soul are separate substances. Labor is always material, in the sense that its real deliberate actions produce real effects, whether or not embodied in objects, this distinction being secondary not primary as those two forms (embodied and not embodied in objects in objects) are complementary to one another, not alternative.

I therefore consider that the movement of bourgeois social thought toward the rejection of labor's central place is the natural accompaniment of the evolution that turned the triumphant bourgeoisie into a new parasitic class. Thenceforward it was the task of this class to find a way to legitimize idleness. To do this they were compelled to believe that proprietorship in and of itself is the source of proprietary incomes. So the bourgeoisie abstracts from the labor that it exploits to put in its place an invented productivity of time or of money: money "gives birth" (which is true for its owner) without any role for labor and production, without which money can have no "offspring." Marx analyzed that mental process as the form of alienation needed for the bourgeoisie to establish its conception of social reality, and for me that analysis has unequalled power.

The title of economist Piero Sraffa's book—*Production of Commodities by Means of Commodities*—is a fine example of such alienation. Lay on the ground all the commodities considered in Sraffa's model—the finished products, raw materials, food for workers' comsumption—and what happens? Obviously nothing without the labor that puts those things together to transform them into each other. The reality is always commodity production with the help of commodities and *labor*.

Contemporary postmodernist rhetorics continue the discourse of that thought, which has to deny reality in order to replace it with the alienated image needed for its representation of the real. For example, to say that contemporary society is one of services and no longer of material production because tourism and out-of-the-home meals are increasing as a share of GDP while manufacturing industry declines makes little sense. When reality is examined beneath its immediate appearance these services require a considerable production of things: no tourism without automobiles, airplanes, roads, and railways; no outside meals without restaurants, foodstuffs, and the like.

The disappearance of labor from the scope of bourgeois social thought, sufficient to term that thought decadent (an adjective I have no hesitation in using), is accompanied by an equally strange discourse on the disappearance of the proletariat. A discourse pronounced at the very moment when the opposite process is taking place: accelerated generalizing of proletarianization. This acceleration takes the form of a generalization of wage labor in the centers and the growth of such labor at dizzying speed in the peripheries. Of course, the new generalized proletariat, confronting the generalized monopolies, is segmented. Among other things, it is divided on the one hand between its preponderant forms in the centers, which are implicitly linked to the modes of control of the worldwide system and to the international division of labor, and on the other hand, to its particular forms in the dominated formations. In the centers, an increasing proportion of workers, sellers of their labor power and thus proletarians, find a place in the economic sectors that secure worldwide domination for the globalized capital of the generalized monopolies: research and development in the fabrication of new needs, information and the deformation of information, finance, and military industries. In the peripheries, there coexist a rapidly growing manufacturing proletariat, an impoverished and oppressed peasantry, and a dizzying growth of the mass of workers in what is called the "informal sector."

What we need is not empty and false chatter about the disappearance of the proletariat but concrete analyses of the generalized proletariat's segmentation. For it is only such analyses that allow movement toward an answer to the sole real question: Can this generalized proletariat develop a class consciousness in the Lukácsian sense of being prepared for the challenge of becoming the universal class, an actor in the project of a classless society, bearer of a communism understood as a higher stage of civilization? I do say "become," since the observation of reality suggests no such thing. The consciousnesses (not consciousness) of belonging to defined social groups (and not to the generalized proletarian class) hold sway. Is it possible to go beyond this infantile stage of social consciousness? Or is that only a utopian (in the banal sense of impossible) wish because it would be foreign to, if not in conflict with, human nature? Bourgeois social thought tries to make us think so, by substituting for Marx's anthropology the anthropology of geneticism or psychologism by way of arguments that seem very weak to me. Marxism, understood not as exegesis of Marx but as the effort to analyze reality critically in order to transform it, seems to me to be by far the most effective toolkit for advancing in response to the challenge, both by thought (inventive and creative in imagination, accurate in concrete analysis) and by action (identification of strategic objectives for the struggle at each stage of its development). Marxism is not outlived; on the contrary, it is more necessary than ever. That does not make me see in Marxism a religion revealed for all time to come. No, by applying Marxism to Marxism we will understand that it will necessarily be surpassed if and when humanity reaches communism, the higher, classless-society stage of civilization. Meanwhile Marxism remains the most effective social thought, therefore the most scientific, for understanding class society and acting to dismantle it.

The divergences thus separating what is produced by the workings of "the market" (a weak term that hides the capitalist relationships framing it) from what the higher logic of social value puts to work do not show Marx's "mistake." On the contrary, they show the whole radical critical bearing of his project, and the success of his demonstration of capitalism's historical nature.

In this study I will put forward an overall picture of the divergences separating the capitalist system's observed system of prices and incomes from one corresponding to such values as those defined by Marx.

The operative forces determining those gaps did not remain unchanged and self-identical throughout the nineteenth and twentieth centuries, and because of this it is important to specify the particular characteristics of each successive phase the capitalist system went through as it unfolded into its finished form, from the Industrial Revolution, starting from the close of the eighteenth century, to our own time, and to identify the nature of the forces to be considered as their activity manifested.

In other respects, these forces show their particular individual aspects according to whether we are dealing with a particular historical social formation (Victorian England, the German Empire from 1870 to 1914, the United States before or after the Civil War, British India, the Ottoman Empire or the Egypt of the nineteenth century, colonial Africa, the countries of today's European Union, or today's emerging countries) or whether we are dealing with the globalized capitalist system at a particular moment of its history (1840, or 1880, or 1930, or 2010). So what counts is to specify the field of play—local or global—in which those different forces operated.

The way in which social value, as formulated by Marx, operates expresses the rationality of a choice of production of definite use-values based on their measure of social utility, which is to say, their usefulness for human society. This rationality transcends such rationality as rules the reproduction of the capitalist mode of production. Capitalist rationality is that which governs the accumulation of capital, based as it is on the extraction of surplus value. Economic decisions are made not by society, but by the capitalists. The system of prices and incomes frames the operative rationality of those decisions. So economic decisions taken in the framework of the empirical system of prices and incomes (themselves defined by the division of the produced value—termed "value added"—between wages and profits) will be different from those that might be made in a framework that respects the demands of the law of social value, which defines, in the coming socialism, the principle of collective social management over economic decisions.

The general social and historical outlook of the bourgeoisie (its *Weltanschauung*) requires belief that capitalism is natural. To that end, bourgeois economic theory attempts to demonstrate that the mode of decision making within the framework of the empirical system of prices and incomes results in a rational allocation of resources (capital and labor) identical to an optimal chosen output of social use values. But it can do so only by way of a succession of tautological arguments involving productivities ascribed to the different "factors of production" (capital and labor), in contrast to Marx's concept of the only existing productivity, that of social labor.

This fundamental difference involving the view of social reality and, consequently, the scientific method needed for its analysis, stems from the contrast between two anthropologies. Marx's conception therefore links the rigorous analysis of the apparent laws governing reproduction of the capitalist mode of production (as given, moreover, at a single moment and place of its spread) to analysis of the totality of forces fashioning social structures and determining their evolution, which make up the object of study for historical materialism.

I will say more about these general conclusions at the end of this essay, which will proceed based on concrete evaluation of the different reasons governing the referred-to system of values/system of prices and incomes divergences, and on evaluation of the functioning of the forces called on to locate and define those reasons.

To start with, I will put forward, pell-mell, a rapid enumeration of the reasons governing those divergences:

1) landed property and rent;
2) control over money capital and the rate of interest;

3) the mobility of capitals and the transformation of values into prices of production;

4) changes, linked to the transformation of capitalism into monopoly capitalism, of the price-determination system;

5) regulation of the price system operative in a monetary system based on commodity money (metal, especially gold);

6) change from that regulation, linked to abandonment of the gold standard;

7) divergence between measurement of social labor as defined in terms of abstract labor and the empirical wage scale;

8) the transformation of the price system required to move from the analysis of a local (national) social formation to that of the global capitalist system linking the dominant central formations to dominated peripheral formations in an unequal interdependence;

9) the effects on the price system of the "financial excrescence," that is, the appraisal of the "value" of a "capital" through that of the stock certificates representing the private appropriation of that "capital" (the quotation marks will be explained further on in my discussion of this matter).

I have already expressed my views on each of those nine selected topics in various old or recent writings. I will recall those writings throughout the following discussions and in the concluding references. But for that reason it seems useful here to put forward a synthesis of them. Each of the reasons for the divergence separating empirical reality from the fundament of the system expressed by the law of social value—in other words, the modus operandi of the latter—is unique.

Some have been working continuously over the course of those two centuries, although in conditions of time and place that shaped the particular ways in which they were expressed. Others appear only with the passage from one stage of capitalist development to the next: especially with the passage from "competitive" (the meaning of the quotation marks will be explained) capitalism to monopoly capitalism, and then from its preliminary form (from 1900 to 1970) to what I call "contemporary capitalism of generalized, financialized, and globalized monopolies" (the meaning of which expression will likewise be explained).

I have adopted a historical presentation of my observations and conclusions, dividing this history among the three successive stages of its unfolding: 1) nineteenth-century competitive capitalism; 2) the primary (1900–1970) stage of monopoly capitalism; 3) contemporary (post-1975) generalized-monopoly capitalism. The advantage of this presentation is to allow articulation of the different mechanisms for those enumerated divergences and to illuminate the holistic nature of their workings: in other words, integrate into a broader historical materialist outlook the economic laws governing each chronologically limited stage of capitalism.

This method can be carried out ad infinitum by looking at slices of time as short as desired and at equally precise localities. To do so would be to write a history of capitalism, and that is not the object of this infinitely more modest work. May the reader excuse what might be considered oversimplifications, which I hope will not be so outrageous as to invalidate its conclusions.

In the course of this short book, I will put special emphasis on the hot subjects that not only have caused critics of Marx to spill much ink but likewise have given rise to stormy debates among Marxists: transformation from value to price, abstract labor, productive and unproductive labor, the law of the tendency of profit, the nature of money, the definition of use value, general economic equilibrium, the question of surplus. The shortness of this work compels me to offer formulations that might well appear brusque, especially to a reader not familiar with the elaborations on these questions that I have made elsewhere and to which I shall make only brief references. In any case, I do not offer them in a polemical spirit. I do not insult those who read Marx differently than I do. I wish only for a deepening of our debates; my only concern is to give an impulse to the struggles for emancipation of workers and peoples.

Nineteenth-Century Competitive Capitalism

The fashionable legend claims that industrial capitalism belongs to an outlived past and that contemporary capitalism henceforward will be based on services and no longer on material production, in place of which would be substituted a capitalism termed cognitive. I will not reiterate here what I have already written about this dubious rhetoric, but not at the price of neglecting the gigantic transformations separating our capitalism from that of the nineteenth century. Perhaps for lack of semantic imagination, I will term nineteenth-century capitalism "concrete" and that of our contemporary world "abstract."

Capitalism, in the completed form it took starting with the Industrial Revolution and in its extension during the nineteenth century, corresponded to a concrete historical reality whose dimensions are crucial to an understanding of its operational logic. The new class, having mastery over economic development and rising steadily to a position of class dominance over the political system, was made up of men and of families linked to determinate and defined economic entities; they were owners of capital (or of its essential elements), of factories, trading houses, specialized financial firms. They made up "concrete bourgeoisies," exercising economic management directly through their private property. This was management through effective competition among capitals (and thus among the capitalists, the bourgeois). This is the concrete competition that Marx analyzes to understand the transformation of the system of values into a system of prices.

Mid-nineteenth-century capitalism, in what Marx knew as the norms and conditions of its establishment in developed Europe (England and Scotland, France, Belgium, the Rhineland, New England), is properly termed "concrete" inasmuch as it was embodied in visible social realities: the bourgeois, himself owner of the physical production sites. Property over means of production grouped in the producing enterprises was personal, familial, or involved only a few associated bourgeois. There were multiple and scattered places in which capitalist production relations were crystallized: there were ironmongers, coal-mine owners, textile mills, trading houses, and banks, each having its unique owner.

Competition among capitalists (and thus among the diversely owned capitals) was real and dependent on two orders of logics. There was competition among firms in the same field, competing in production of use values: competition within groups of spinners, weavers, coal mines, trading houses. This competition forced them into innovative techniques of production: the introduction of more efficient machines and more effective ways to organize labor. But it must be recognized that the rationality of this calculation, aiming to reduce the production cost for each unit of use value output, does not produce the same results as those that would stem from a calculation whose objective would be to reduce the social cost of that output as measured by the quantity of abstract social labor expended to that purpose.

But there was likewise competition among branches producing different use values. Surplus value, proportional to the volume of direct labor put to work, was to take form as profit through the division of capitals among branches of production of differing organic composition, that is, of different ratios of constant (non-labor inputs) to variable capital (labor). This was the notorious transformation of values into prices of production.

Marx deals with these two fields of competition among capitals, which enable the passage from values to prices of production and to market prices. That treatment calls for specifications about the nature of Marx's project, the productivity of social labor, the question of the transformation of values into prices of production, the concept of abstract labor, and the trend over time of the rate of profit.

Marx's Project

Marx's project, in his critical analysis of capital, was to separate out the mode of operation of the capitalist law of value masked by the appearance of the workings of markets. That choice is obviously incomprehensible to bourgeois economics, which, in its characteristic spirit of formal logic and empiricist positivism, thinks it can directly grasp "reality."

Marx's project is of another sort, to be grasped only by understanding the meaning of *Capital*'s subtitle, *Critique of Political Economy*. This critique consists not in substituting a "good economic theory" for another one judged bad or inadequate, but in shining light on the status of this new science. Marx is answering a new question, put by him alone: In what kind of society is this new economic science the product? What social vision allowed it to emerge, and what are the limits within which that vision confines it? Marx discovered the specific nature of capitalism, in contrast to the ways in which earlier societies were organized. This nature inheres in the fact that the economic factor is not merely "determining in the last resort" but that it becomes the directly dominant factor. Because of this, economics becomes independent, freeing itself from its previous subordination to the political/ideological factor characteristic of previous regimes. Economic and mercantile alienation, proper to capitalism, now gives a new status—that of an objective reality governed by "laws" working in society like external forces—to the practices governing the reproduction of the economic system. The space is cleared for constitution of a new science, whose aim is to discover those "laws."

Marx's ambition, beyond discovery of those "laws," was wider yet. He aimed to place those apparent laws governing capitalism in a more ample historical panorama, transcending capitalism. To do that, he had to go roundabout, by way of the analysis of social labor and of value. This detour allowed him to understand how under capitalism social labor takes on forms different from those expressed in previous periods, how under capitalism social labor is dominated by capital (exploited) and how the apparent laws governing accumulation (the appreciation of capital) conceal that domination.

In other words, how the product of the exploitation of social labor takes the form of profits for different segments of capital and of property owned and controlled by the new, bourgeois dominating class. The transformation of values into prices is at the heart of that analysis.

The Productivity of Social Labor

In Marx's analysis, there exists only one "productivity," which is social labor defined by the quantities of abstract labor contained in the commodity product turned out by a collective of workers.

The productivity of social labor is improved whenever society, to produce a definite unit of use value, can devote to that end a lesser quantity of abstract (direct and indirect) labor. Such improvement is the result of progress in the technologies put into operation on the basis of society's scientific knowledge. The productivities of social labor can be compared in two production units outputting the same use value; it is meaningless to compare productivities of social labor in two branches of production outputting different use values. So comparing the general productivity of social labor in two successive periods of capitalist development (or, more broadly, of historical development), or of two systems (two countries, for example), occurs through analogical reasoning. The measurement of this general productivity is obtained by calculating the weighted average of progress in productivity in the different branches of production of analogous use values. This is an approximate calculation, since the number of use values in the total to be considered is always much higher than the number that can be taken into account and the weighting itself is in part dependent on the evolution of productivities in each of the branches considered.

As I have said, the law of value formulated by Marx, based on the concept of abstract labor, expresses the rationality of the social utility of a definite use value. This rationality is not that which governs the reproduction, ordered by the extraction of surplus value, of the capitalist mode of production. Although the system of values is independent of the rate of extraction of surplus value, the system of prices itself is inseparable from the distribution of incomes, Piero Sraffa failed in his attempt to define a unit of measure that would let him free the price structure from its dependance in regard to distribution.

Bourgeois economic theory, which claims that the market through which prices are expressed produces a rational allocation of resources, arrives at this notion only by artificially carving up productivity into "components" ascribed to each of the "factors of production." Although this partitioning is devoid of scientific value and is based merely on tautological arguments, it is "useful" because it is the only way to legitimize capital's profit. The method utilized by this bourgeois economics to determine the "wage," as the marginal productivity of the "last worker hired," stems from the same tautology and shatters the unity of the collective, the only creator of value. Moreover, contrary to the unproven assertions of conventional economics, employers do not make their decisions by way of this "marginal calculation."

Progress in the productivity of social labor expresses itself through reduction in the quantity of abstract labor needed to produce one unit of the same use value. So it is necessary to identify this unit. Empirically, this is surely not too difficult: meters of cloth, or tons of cement, an automobile of a given horsepower, so many hours of babysitting, a particular type of doctor's examination, etc. To grasp the progress of productivity for their production is generally easy in the short to medium term (up to a few years). This year's model of an automobile has a use value analogous to that of last year. We thus can measure the gain in productivity from one year to another, and going back in time by short stages—in economic calculation this is called measurement "in constant prices"—conclude that productivity has doubled over, say, thirty years. But by going back in time this way, the changes that define the use value at issue are ignored. Take, for example, transportation. By airplane, a human being can be carried a distance of 15,000 km in one day. A hundred and fifty years ago, to cover that distance by coach and sailing ship would have taken a full year, 365 times as long. Can one say that the airplane is 365 times more efficacious (and treat that effectiveness as productivity) than the coach-ship complex of yesteryear? Or should one compare the duration of social labor needed today to produce an airplane (and divide that time by the number of passenger-kilometers transported in one year) to that which was necessary in that time to produce the coach and the ship (divided in like fashion)? This is an exercise that is nearly impossible, and moreover is useless, because the use values at issue are no longer the same, nor the needs underlying them.

Marx pointed out, rightly, that consumption modes are not prior givens in regard to production decisions, but that, contrariwise, it is production that gives its orders to consumption.

In some domains measurement of "productivity gains" is even more problematic, conventional, even illusory and deceptive, because the use values being compared are not comparable. Can one say that today's medicine is "one-and-a-half times" as efficacious or "productive" as that of a century ago if, over that span, longevity has increased by 50 percent? For example, the increasing cost of health is measured, from year to year, as its percentage of the total expenditures making up the GDP. But it is known that the same proportions of the latter (comparable between the United States and Western Europe) give different outcomes. So there are other criteria of social choice that cannot be reduced to the choices set forth by supposed economic (capitalist in this case) rationality.

The Transformation Problem

Much ink has been spilled on account of the transformation problem. Transformation indeed involves a necessary difference between the rate of profit as measured in the system of prices of production and that drawn from the system of values. This discrepancy has been treated by economists as proof of the failure of Marx's conception of transformation. In contradistinction, I have said and repeated that this difference was, to the contrary, expectable and necessary for anyone who does not, miles away from Marx's thought and from his distinction between immediate phenomenal appearances and the essential material reality behind them, reduce scientific analysis to direct empirical observation. If the two rates of profit at issue were identical, the exploitation of labor in the forms characteristic of capitalism would be as transparent as it was in previous epochs. A serf works three days on his land and three on that of his lord; the rate of surplus labor drawn from the serf's exploitation is immediately visible. Under capitalism exploitation is made opaque by the generalized commodity form of social relationships: the proletarian sells his labor power, not his labor. That opacity is given expression by the difference between the two rates.

The analysis, then, of the realization conditions for expanded accumulation that Marx carries out in the second volume of *Capital*, is based, quite logically, on the distinction between two departments of production, one the producer of capital goods, the other of consumer goods. This analysis centers its attention on the segment of the productive system directly governed by the capitalist mode. It is not a matter of a theory of general supply/demand equilibrium comparable and analogous to those (Walrasian or Sraffian) of bourgeois economics. For in its evolution, the rate of surplus value is subject to the results of working-class struggles and to the mode of expansion of the capitalist segment of the productive system, which absorbs (or subordinates) the other (peasant and artisan) forms of commodity production. As a whole, the system does not tend toward an equilibrium that can be predefined but rather goes from disequilibrium to disequilibrium. Marx's analysis, unlike that of bourgeois economics, is not economic determinist; its place is in the much wider field of historical materialism.

Marx had built his critique of capitalism, and of the economic theory legitimizing its extension, during the competitive-capitalism epoch of the nineteenth century. The theory of value and that of the transformation of the system of values into a system of prices made up the central axis of that critique. Bourgeois economists before Marx (the vulgar economics of Say, Bastiat et al.) and above all after him put their efforts to an attempted demonstration that subjection of society to the requirements of generalized competitive markets would result in a general equilibrium favoring progress for all, at national and global levels. The two great attempts at such a demonstration (by Walras and by Sraffa) failed to do so (see my book *The Law of World-wide Value*). Moreover, the reality of the global system has shown that capitalism does not result in homogenization of economic conditions at that level but, on the contrary, produces increasing polarization.

The Concept of Abstract Labor

The concept of abstract labor, formulated by Marx, defines the common denominator allowing the addition of different forms of simple (unskilled) and complex (skilled) labor. The unit of abstract labor is a composite unit linking, in given proportions, units of simple (without skill) and complex (skilled) labor. Simple (unskilled) and complex (requiring training) labor are easy to understand. But the concept of abstract labor is not directly visible. Now, the products of a society are not the work of laborers isolated from each other but of a collective, apart from which neither the least skilled nor the most highly skilled labor has any meaning: their contributions together are what make those products.

Can an hour worked by an engineer and one by a laborer be regarded as contributing equal amounts to the produced value? And if not, in what proportions? Bourgeois economics, ignoring value through confusing it with (what is called market) price, dodges the question: for it, the different wages of the engineer and the laborer reflect the unequal social utility of their contributions. Which is to beg the question with a pure and simple tautology, putting recognition in place of explanation.

I have proposed a way to calculate the proportions ordering the differing contributions to value formation, based on accounting for the training time needed to produce skilled workers and recovery of the cost of such training over the working life of such a skilled worker. This method would justify a wage ratio (skilled wage divided by unskilled wage) of one to one and a half or two, hardly more. This method seems to me to be consonant with that of Marx and would allow reduction of complex (skilled) labor to simple labor. (I refer the reader to Part Three of this book for details.)

Now, the empirical wage scale is much broader than that which would be suggested by the operations of the abstract-labor concept. Thus, this concept does not explain the empirical wage scale deriving, in the world such as it is, from the long history of inequality and differently valued social statuses, and from the relative poverty (remaining even in the rich countries) of shareable wealth. The attempt to legitimize this hierarchy as expressing the marginal productivities of the work done by different categories of worker is tautological. Capitalism's ideology always valorizes inequality, whether of wages or as expressed in capital wealth, by arguments that make inequality the source of progress. Reality makes clear that solidarity has a more important role, in achieving not only social progress (trade unions) but also, likewise, the progress of sciences and technologies in all historical ages.

If the wage scale for different categories of skilled workers extends over a broad span, going, let us say, from 1.5 to 2 times subsistence (the unskilled wage) for many, 3 to 4 times for some, and a much higher multiple for a small minority termed "extra-skilled," it will be recognized that though the majority of workers contribute to the formation of surplus value, albeit in differing proportions—and in this sense the expression "super-exploited" in regard to the two-thirds majority of wage earners is quite meaningful—there exists also a category of the supposed "super-skilled" (and they may sometimes really be so) who consume more surplus value than that to which their labor contributes.

An empiricist mind might believe that the unit of abstract labor can be calculated on the basis of the observed wage scale by taking the weighted average of actual wages. For my part, I consider this operation forbidden by the concept of abstract labor. The observed divergence is no proof of Marx committing yet another logical error; on the contrary, the recognition of this divergence allows location of the relativity of the supposed rationality of class society.

Capitalism's characteristic fundamental inequality in the distribution of income rests in the first instance on the contrast opposing the power of the owners of capital to the subordination of the sellers of labor power. The wage scale comes as a supplement. But the latter has acquired a new dimension. The contemporary system of generalized-monopoly capital is based on extreme centralization in the control of capital, accompanied by a generalization of wage labor. In these conditions a large fraction of profit is disguised in the form of wages (or quasi-wages) of the higher levels of the middle classes who are employed as servants of capital. Thus the separations among the formation of value, the extraction of surplus-value, and the distribution of the surplus value become yet wider.

But what of the hierarchy of remunerations in a distant future? In that future will there still have to be engineers and laborers? The materialist dialectic of the coming evolution will give its answer to the question and at present the diverse possibilities can only be glimpsed by imagination alone. Reflection on that question illuminates the fallacious character of ascribing an absolute character to the capitalist system's rationality. The bourgeois economist's absolute rationality becomes relative in the temporal space extending beyond capitalism as a historical phase. On that scale it can even become irrationality, as we will see, for example, in dealing with natural resources.

Trending Evolution of the Rate of Profit

Marx's schemas of expanded reproduction allow quantitative specification of the rate of growth in wages needed for the realization of accumulation, a rate that is defined by the rates of productivity growth in each of the two departments, I and II. If this condition is fulfilled, the rate of profit is in turn defined and, as I have shown elsewhere, does not necessarily exhibit a downward tendency. That would require an increase in the organic composition of capital expressed in a price of production linked to a rate of surplus value that is not itself increasing notably.

Is Marx's intuition, suggesting that such is the case, well founded? Yes, insofar as increasing productivity involves not production of the same capital goods in increasing quantity (the model of extensive growth without progress in productivity) but innovation, that is, the production of new capital goods. At the same time the extension of capitalist social relations, the relationships through which the power of capital is expressed, reduces the capability of workers to gain the level of wage increases required to assure the dynamic equilibrium of accumulation. Thus the major countertendency to the fall in the rate of profit is at work in a real way. In short, the history of accumulation exhibits successive phases, sometimes marked by a falling tendency of the rate of profit, as was the case during the "Thirty Glorious Years" of the postwar period when the working classes were benefiting from considerable political power, sometimes marked by a recovery in the rate of profit as in the decades 1980 to 2010. But then this recovery caused a problem for realization of the general supply/demand equilibrium in regard to consumer goods. The movement of this contradiction, inherent to capitalism, cannot be explained solely by the play of economic laws but by the relationship of the latter to the results of the class struggle. Bourgeois economics ignores this dialectic, to which Marx gives its proper rank.

The Question of Land Rents and the Interest on Money Capital

In the nineteenth century's competitive capitalism divergences between the system of values and that of prices and incomes are beyond those associated with the transformation of values into prices of production. In *Capital* Marx discusses two of those divergences, linked in one case to land rents and in the other to interest on money capital.

I have dared to call into question the economic theory of land rent, which Marx bases on the differences in organic composition of capital between agriculture and industry. Besides, Marx forgets about this theory when he shifts the emphasis of his analysis to the questions of historical materialism posed in their connection: the class conflicts and alliances linking great landowners to peasants within different forms of anti-working-class alliance.

The topic of interest raises questions relating to the functions of the monetary system and of the state, to which I will return further on.

The Twentieth Century's Initial Monopoly Capitalism (1900–1975)

Neither Marx nor even the main late-nineteenth-century Marxist thinkers believed for a moment that the system as it existed in their epoch made up a definitive structure. On the contrary, they accentuated the tendencies of its evolution ordered by the unfolding of its logic. With remarkable intuition, Marx noted the importance of the initial manifestations of the transformations in the form of capital ownership: the establishment of the first joint-stock corporations in the priority areas requiring assemblage of a large mass of capital (railroads and mines). At the time, all the Marxists predicted that forms of small commodity production would inevitably disappear and be absorbed into expanding capital. And even though the formulation of their vision of this programmed disappearance turned out to be wrong (in particular, see what Kautsky had to say about the future of agricultural production), the idea on which their vision was based—the concentration/centralization of capital, resulting from competition that is doomed to dialectical self-negation—was confirmed by history. So that when, at the end of the nineteenth century, Hobson and Hilferding undertook analyses of the new monopoly capitalism there was nothing surprising about it for the period's Marxists.

The first long systemic crisis of capitalism got under way in the 1870s. The version of historic capitalism's extension over the long span that I have put forward suggests a succession of three epochs: ten centuries of incubation from the year 1000 in China to the eighteenth-century revolutions in England and France, a short century of triumphal flourishing (the nineteenth century), probably a long decline comprising in itself the first long crisis (1875–1945) and then the second (begun in 1975 and still ongoing). In each of those two long crises capital responded to the challenge by the same triple formula: concentration of capital's control, deepening of uneven globalization, and financialization of the system's management.

Two major thinkers, Hobson and Hilferding, immediately grasped the enormous importance of capitalism's transformation into monopoly capitalism. No surprise that the former be British, from the nineteenth century's hegemonic power, nor that in his analysis he would place special emphasis on the forms of the new financialization of the system. No more surprising is it that the latter be Austro-German, the German Empire then being embarked on an accelerated industrialization actively supported by the state and the nascent monopolies, favored by the large monetary indemnity imposed on France.

But it was up to Lenin to draw the political conclusion from this transformation, which began the decline of capitalism and thus the inscription of socialist revolution on the order of the day. Lenin was pretty much the only one to have seen that the powers' monopoly capitalism was pregnant with world war, the opportunity for revolution.

The same evolution—the formation of monopoly capitalism—was under way on the other side of the Atlantic. The Yankee victory in the Civil War had put an end to a system of power until then largely under the sway of the South's landowner/slaveowner aristocracies. And the last quarter-century's prodigious industrial expansion was conducive to the invention of new forms of monopoly, the only way to enable continuation of its extension.

The primary formation of monopoly capitalism thus goes back to the end of the nineteenth century, but in the United States it really established itself as a system only in the 1920s, to conquer next the Western Europe and Japan of the "Thirty Glorious Years" following the Second World War. The concept of surplus, put forth by Paul Baran and Paul Sweezy in the 1950–60 decade, allows a grasp of what is essential in the transformation of capitalism brought about by the dominant emergence of the monopolies. Convinced as I was by that work of enrichment to the Marxist critique of capitalism, I undertook as soon as the 1970s its reformulation, which required, in my opinion, the transformation of the "first" (1920–70) monopoly capitalism into generalized-monopoly capitalism, analyzed as a qualitatively new phase of the system.

In the previous forms of competition among firms producing the same use value—numerous then, and independent of one another—decisions were made by the capitalist owners of those firms on the basis of a recognized market price that imposed itself as an external datum. Baran and Sweezy observed that the new monopolies acted differently: they set their prices simultaneously with the nature and volume of their outputs. So it was an end to "fair and open competition," which remains, quite contrary to reality, at the heart of conventional economics rhetoric. The abolition of competition, the radical transformation of that term's meaning, of its functioning and of its results, detaches the price system from its basis, the system of values, and in that very way hides from sight the referential framework that used to define capitalism's rationality. Although use values once constituted to a great extent autonomous realities, they become, in monopoly capitalism, the object of actual fabrications produced systematically through aggressive and particularized sales strategies (advertising, brands, etc.).

In monopoly capitalism a coherent reproduction of the productive system is no longer possible merely by mutual adjustment of the two departments discussed in volume 2 of *Capital*: it is thenceforward necessary to take into account a Department III, conceived by Baran and Sweezy, of surplus absorption. I have tried to make an estimate of this Department III that reflects the really observed evolution of the composition of the overall output of the economies at issue over the course of the twentieth century. I thus refer the reader to that illustration of the modus operandi of monopoly capitalism, which a reading of Baran and Sweezy inspired me to write (see Part Two).

The excrescence of Department III, in turn, favors, in fact, the erasure of the distinction made by Marx between productive surplus-value-producing labor and unproductive labor. All forms of wage labor can become, and do become, sources of possible profits. A hairdresser sells his services to a customer who pays him out of his income. But if that hairdresser becomes the employee of a beauty parlor, the business must realize a profit for its owner. Exploited labor is no longer only that of the producers of surplus value, as I recalled in the comments I put forth regarding the patchwork makeup of Department III. If the country at issue puts ten million wage workers to work in Departments I, II, and III, providing the equivalent of twelve million years of abstract labor, and if the wages received by those workers allow them to buy goods and services requiring merely six million years of abstract labor, the rate of exploitation for all of them, productive and unproductive confounded, is the same 100 percent. But the six million years of abstract labor that the workers do not receive cannot all be invested in the purchase of producer goods destined to the expansion of Departments I and II; part of them will have to be put toward the expansion of Department III.

Generalized Monopoly Capitalism since 1975

Passage from initial monopoly capitalism to its current form (generalized-monopoly capitalism) was accomplished in a short time (between 1975 and 2000) in response to the second long crisis of declining capitalism. In fifteen years, monopoly power's centralization and its capacity for control over the entire productive system reached summits incomparable with what had until then been the case.

My first formulation of generalized-monopoly capitalism dates from 1978, when I put forward an interpretation of capital's responses to the challenge of its long systemic crisis, which opened starting in 1971 to 1975. In that interpretation I accentuated the three directions of this expected response, then barely under way: strengthened centralization of control over the economy by the monopolies, deepening of globalization (and the outsourcing of manufacturing industry toward the peripheries), and financialization. The work that André Gunder Frank and I published together in 1978 drew no notice, probably because our theses were ahead of their time. But today the three characteristics at issue have become blindingly obvious to everybody.[1]

A name had to be given to this new phase of monopoly capitalism. "Late monopoly capitalism"? I thought that the adjective "late," sort of like the prefix "post," ought to be avoided because by itself it gives no positive indication about the content and full significance of the novel features. The adjective "generalized" specifies this: the monopolies are thenceforward in a position giving them the capability of reducing all (or nearly all) economic activities to subcontractor status. The example of family farming in the capitalist centers provides the finest example of this.

These farmers are controlled upstream by the monopolies that provide their inputs and financing, downstream by the marketing chains, to the point that the price structures forced on them wipe out the income from their labor. Farmers only survive thanks to public subsidies paid for by the taxpayers. This extraction is thus at the origin of the monopolies' profits. As has been observed likewise with bank failures, the new principle of economic management is summed up in a phrase: privatization of the monopolies' profits, socialization of their losses. To go on talking of "fair and open competition" and of "truth of the prices revealed by the markets" belongs in a farce. But economists have no sense of humor, and the persistence they show in carrying on the study of an imaginary system that has nothing to do with reality qualifies them for the Nobel Prizes handed out to them!

The fragmented, and by that fact concrete, economic power of proprietary bourgeois families gives way to a centralized power exercised by the directors of the monopolies and their cohort of salaried servitors. For generalized-monopoly capitalism involves not the concentration of property, which on the contrary is more dispersed than ever, but the power to manage it. That is why it is deceptive to attach the adjective "patrimonial" to contemporary capitalism. It is only in appearance that shareholders rule. Absolute monarchs, the top executives of the monopolies decide everything in their name. In turn, that management wipes out the former modus operandi of competition among capitals, which used to constitute the basis for the way in which capital accumulation was regulated. It puts in its place a way of management based on alternation between negotiated cooperation and brutal competition among monopolies (which works through methods that are not those of the "fair and open competition" in which we are supposed to believe). Power, in the most abstract sense of the term, takes the place of concrete effective competition. Moreover, the deepening globalization of the system wipes out the holistic—that is, simultaneously economic, political, and social—logic of national systems without putting in its place any global logic whatsoever. This is the "empire of chaos" (title of one of my works, published in 1991, and subsequently taken up by others). In fact international political violence takes the place of economic competition, while the discourse seeks to make us believe that regulation of the system results from this.[2]

The New System: Prices and Incomes
Disconnected from Values

The concept of generalized-monopoly capitalism allows us to locate the significance of the major transformations involving the configuration of class structures and the ways in which political life is managed in the centers and in the peripheries.

In the system's centers (the Triad of United States, Western Europe, and Japan), generalized-monopoly capitalism has brought with it generalization of the wage form. The so-called upper managers, linked to management of the economy by the monopolies, are thenceforward employees who do not participate in the formation of surplus value, of which they have become consumers, deserving by that fact to be characterized as a component sector of the bourgeoisie. At the other social pole, the generalized proletarianization that the wage form suggests is accompanied by a multiplication in the forms of segmentation of the labor force. In other words, the proletariat, in its forms as known in the past, disappears at the very moment when proletarianization becomes generalized.

In the peripheries—as always extremely diverse since they are only defined negatively, as regions that have not become established as centers of the global system—the (direct or indirect) effects of domination by generalized-monopoly capital are no less visible. Above the diversity both of local ruling classes and statuses of subordinate classes is the power of a dominant super-class emerging in the wake of globalization. This super-class is sometimes that of "comprador insiders," sometimes that of the governing political class (or class-state-party), or a mixture of the two.

The power of domination of the economy by generalized-monopoly capitalism has required and made possible the transformation of the forms in which political life is managed. In the centers, a new political consensus culture synonymous with depoliticization, has taken the place of the political culture based on the right-left confrontation that used to give significance to bourgeois democracy and the contradictory inscription of class struggles within its framework. Far from being synonyms, "market," that is, the "non-market" that characterizes management of the economy by the generalized monopolies, and "democracy" are antonyms. In the peripheries, the monopoly of power captured by the dominant local super-class, which I refer to in my 2013 book, *The Implosion of Contemporary Capitalism*, likewise involves the negation of democracy.[3] This, in turn, fortifies forms of depoliticization, forms that are diverse but whose effects are quite the same. I have tried to provide an example appropriate to those countries that are victims of the rise of political Islam.

Domination by the capital of the generalized monopolies is exercised on the world scale through global integration of the monetary and financial market, based on the principle of flexible exchange rates, abandonment of the gold standard, and giving up national controls over the flow of capital. Nevertheless, this domination is called into question, to varying degrees, by state policies of the emerging countries. The conflict between these policies and the strategic objectives of the Triad's collective imperialism becomes by that fact one of the central axes for possibly putting generalized-monopoly capitalism once more on trial.

The new financialization of economic life crowns this transformation in capital's power. In place of the concrete forms of its expression is abstract affirmation of the power of capital. Instead of strategies set out by real owners of fragmented capital, we have those of the managers of ownership titles over capital. What is vulgarly called fictitious capital (the estimated value of ownership certificates) is nothing but the expression of this displacement, this disconnect between the virtual and real worlds.

The abstract character of contemporary capital is synonymous with permanent, insurmountable, chaos. By its very nature capitalist accumulation has always been synonymous with disorder, in the sense that Marx gave to that term:

a system moving from disequilibrium to disequilibrium, driven by class struggles and conflicts among the Powers, without ever tending toward an equilibrium. But this disorder resulting from competition among fragmented capitals was kept within reasonable limits through management of the credit system carried out under the control of the national state. With abstract contemporary capitalism, those frontiers disappear; the violence of the movements from disequilibrium to disequilibrium is reinforced. The successor of disorder is chaos.

Bourgeois economic theory endeavors to try to answer the challenge of chaos by denying its existence. To do that, it continues its conventional discourse, which talks of "fair and open competition," nonexistent in fact, and of "true prices." One talks of "less state" although the public-sector share of GDP not only never has been so large but also constitutes the condition *sine qua non* for survival of the system! But in parallel to this empty and unreal discourse, the theory claims to reconstruct the (false) theorem of market self-regulation by shifting the analysis of economic decision making, attributed without proof to individuals, to their expectations. Thus the circle is closed: economic theory, still that of an imaginary system (and not that of real capitalism) is, to boot, one enabling foresight of anything and everything as a function of expectations whose conformity to reality remains forever unknown. Economic theory is, more than ever, an ideological discourse, in the most negative sense of the term, aimed at forcing acceptance of decisions made by the only deciders: the generalized monopolies.

Regulation of Capitalism by the State
and the Credit System

Struggles and alliances among classes, competition among capitals, and conflicts among the powers—realities that all belong to the domain of historical materialism and for that reason cannot be reduced to workings of economic law as suggested by conventional economics—thus result in a system that moves from disequilibrium to disequilibrium without ever tending toward an equilibrium that can in advance be defined in economic terms. By nature, capitalism is an unstable system. Thus the disorder that characterizes it is a reality that cannot be gotten rid of by any economistic reduction.

This disorder, nevertheless, is successfully regulated, often (but not always) by national state policies mobilizing, on one hand, the systematic construction of hegemonic social blocs, and on the other, national management of the system of money and of credit. State and money together make up the means utilized to overcome the disorder resulting from the conflicts of interest among capitals, that is, capital whose ownership is segmented. The state thus often acts "against" the interests of capitalists at odds with one another, in order that the interests of capitalism prevail.

This way of regulation was based, in the nineteenth century, on adoption of metal as a money commodity, with bimetallism evolving toward gold monometallism. This system rules out the possibility of financing inflation through uncontrolled credit expansion. To this end, I distinguish the large waves of price change linked to those ordering gold production from true inflation, which is a subsequent phenomenon. In this connection I have adopted Marx's analyses concerning the relations between gold production and the demand for money; I have extended his arguments by my proposition of an "active role of credit" in accumulation as an answer to Rosa Luxemburg's observations on the realization of surplus value. Here I refer the reader to my book: *Unequal Development.*[4]

It is indeed quite possible to compute the amount of credit that must of necessity be advanced to capitalists at the start of each production cycle for surplus value to be realized and the loans repaid at the end of the cycle. The rate of growth of this amount of credit is itself calculable; it is a function of the rate of growth of GDP and the growth rates of productivity in each of the Departments I and II. This reckoning gives objective status to the concept of demand for money called on by Marx against quantity theories of money. It gives its full meaning to Marx's affirmation that demand for money creates its supply. The possible effectiveness of the credit system is thus not a stylistic approximation but a concrete precise reality that I have termed "the active function of money in accumulation." The proposed method, derived from Marx's reproduction schemata in *Capital*, volume 2, makes explicit that which Marx had left vague and uncalculated. Unfortunately, Marxists are too often content with nothing more than doing exegeses of Marx. By that they have even weakened his argument, which, extended as I do, annihilates the validity of any monetarist theory, previous or contemporary.

The efficacity of the credit system, its capacity to fulfill correctly the requirements of accumulation, obviously depends on conditions that have to be specified. This policy can be, and generally was, efficacious as long as it was working within the framework of a self-centered national productive system. And, in that sense, money and state are inseparable, which was the case until the 1970s. It is no longer so since the national state gave up fulfilling its role in regulating accumulation by regulating credit, without a supranational state taking up the task, and since, in parallel, national management of the monetary system gave way to the vagaries of a globalized and integrated monetary and financial system. This setting adrift, forced by the generalized monopolies raising themselves to the rank of sole actor, led me to conclude that we are dealing with an unviable, naturally chaotic system. The deviation involves not only the global system; in the same way, it involves the European subsystem and that of the euro, based on the same principles. The ongoing implosion of the euro stands witness to that.

The new strategy of the dominant monopoly-capitalist firms was scarcely reconcilable with nineteenth-century techniques of managing capitalism, based on the gold standard system.

Also, the disappearance from sight of the fundamental reference points established by values was concomitant with the progressive abandonment of historic capitalism's other solid point of reference—commodity money (metal, gold)—an abandonment started by the chaos of the First World War. The attempt to return to gold during the interwar period malfunctioned. The solution provided by the Bretton Woods system (1945–71) was effective only insofar as the United States by itself took on the functions of the hegemonic economy (the dollar-based gold exchange standard), and it disappeared in 1971 when the international convertibility of the dollar into gold was terminated. Since then, floating exchange rates have introduced yet another ground for permanent chaos.

The loss of the reference point constituted by metallic money implies a critique of the logic of accumulation. That loss of reference brought about the appearance of a new way to manage accumulation, linked to the disorder of thenceforward possible inflation. Currently, the affirmed will to preclude any inflationary outlook, still without a return to metallic money but by carrying out permanent deflationary monetary policies (a will affirmed more by Germany than by others) calls for a reconsideration and deepening of the concept of money in capitalism. Losing sight of the solid reference point of metallic money might have been compensated for by centralized management of credit, carried out by the state. In part, this solution was utilized throughout the thirty "glorious" postwar years. The system's entry, starting in 1975, into crisis and the response given in terms of deepening globalization (and for Europe a construction inscribed into the globalization at issue) led the state to abandon this management of credit and to yield it to the monopolies' direct power. But the resulting stagnation and chaos have put the gold fetish back in the saddle, showing in this way the inseparability of economistic alienation from the permanence of an indispensable fetish.

National methods of regulating competitive capitalism, and even monopoly capitalism in its primary form, were effective, and were expressed in the succession of expansionary phases and of phases of readjustment via crisis that make up the economic cycle.

Living and Dead Labor, the Time Factor, Discounting the Future, and the Rate of Interest

The law of value involves the possibility of summing quantities of living and of dead labor. Bourgeois economics deals with this matter by introducing time into its argument: capi-tal equipment is first produced, then used. This, of course, is obvious. But behind this treatment can be seen an ethical a priori: saving must first occur before there can be investment. And as long as this is so, the income on capital (equated to capital equipment) finds its justification in the sacrifice represented by saving, a sacrifice defined by the price of time, which is termed discount of the future. The triteness of the argument stems from an identification between individual behavior and the reality of social function. An individual with foresight saves first, invests next. Puritan morality shines through the praise of such behavior. It is next transposed to the collectivity: the nation must save in order to invest. Poli-ticians, right-wingers and social democrats alike, repeat it in accord with one another.

Now, at the scale of the reality of the capitalist mode of production, things do not happen that way. The production of means of production and means of consumption is concomi-tant, it orders a social division of labor between Departments I and II. Expanded reproduction involves Department I pro-ducing a surplus beyond mere replacement of depreciated equipment. Time is indeed taken into account, since that sur-plus will be used in the next phase of production, but not in the way it is in the puritan argument referred to above. For it is the decision to invest (to have Department I produce more than needed to cover depreciation) that creates saving, which does not precede investment but follows from it. Keynes as well as Marx recognized the fallacy involved in treating indivi-dual (micro) behavior as the same as social (macro) behavior.

Here again, the contrast between the system's claimed absolute rationality and its necessary relativization shows itself in full daylight. Investment decisions are not taken collectively; they result from competition that forces firms to plan their modernization and expansion, thus creating a potential demand for capital equipment exceeding the requirements of depreciation. Expanded reproduction results from the rationality of the system, which seems absolute. Raised to the higher level, represented by society (which is not to be reduced to the entrepreneurial class), the rationality of investment decisions ought to be ordered according to other criteria, relativizing the criteria ordering capitalist reproduction. Considerations about the use of natural resources, which we will come to further on, will have to find their place identified among those criteria, though they are ignored by the falsely absolute rationality of bourgeois economics. In the same way, from a social point of view, the generations of youth in training, of active workers, and of pensioners must be considered as solidary elements composing the same society and not as entities competing with one another.

How Does Marx Take Account of Time
in Economic Calculation?

Bourgeois economics treats the rate by which the future is discounted as a component of the interest rate, which is also and simultaneously the price paid for acquiring the advantage of liquidity. The rate of profit—itself the sum of the rate of interest and a supposed "risk premium"—is by that very fact defined in temporal terms: the annual profit returned by capital.

With a clear conscience Marx ignores the concept of discounting the future. He puts forth his own treatment of interest in the framework of the redistribution of surplus value. Nevertheless, Marx integrates time into his analysis of capitalist economic calculation, whose logic, that of a system guided by maximization of capital's annual rate of profit, he carefully restores. The times needed for production, for the circulation of capital, and for the realization of the product undergo a constant pressure tending toward their reduction. The procedures put into operation with this in mind produce effects of redistribution of surplus value in the course of its transformation into profit.

But what of longer time spans? Here we again come upon the challenges of social rationalities transcending those of capitalist management. Among others, precisely, are those of dealing with the "long or very long-term" effects of the choices of social logic. In times to come, we will perhaps conceive an "appreciation of the future" rather than its discounting.

At the Borders of the Capitalist Mode of Production

Marx, who carried out his research by starting from the visible concrete and rising to the level of the abstract, proceeds in the opposite direction to present their results. Thus *Capital* begins with an exposition of the essence of the mode of production grasped at the highest level of abstraction, which can be termed "pure capitalism," reduced to two classes and a single mode of labor—wage labor. In the system of capitalist production, taken at that level of abstraction, Marx's distinction between productive labor, paid out of variable capital, and unproductive labor, paid for by the spending of income, takes on great importance: productive labor is termed such because it alone produces surplus value. In contrast, the work of state employees, providers of public services, like that of private providers of services paid for out of personal incomes, has no part in the extraction of surplus-value—it provides for its redistribution.

But obviously the real concrete capitalist society—the capitalist formations—can never be reduced to a "pure" mode of production. And when Marx comes down to the concrete, it was obviously to what was concrete in his epoch. In the nineteenth century capitalist production relations occupied a limited space in the totality of production relations: the domains ruled by peasant and artisanal production still take up a large part of the terrain, and preserve a measure of still-active effective autonomy even as their subordination to the dominant logics of capital accumulation continually increase.

The importance of this observation stems from the fact that the expansion of capitalist relations will take place in the nineteenth century precisely through the destruction or absorption, or formal subordination, of the earlier forms, a process that gives to the capitalism of the epoch its triumphant character synonymous with progress, as the sentences of the *Communist Manifesto* bear witness. And it is for this reason that I have given a reading of the expansion of capitalism that reduces the progressive phase of the system to that short nineteenth century. Rosa Luxemburg had given proof of a fine intuition when she insisted on the importance for expanded reproduction of the absorption or subordination of non-capitalist forms of production. Her arguments about the role of imperialist capitalism's expansion in the colonies and semi-colonies of the fin de siècle can be transferred, mutatis mutandis, to the conditions of capital's internal expansion in the countries of Europe between 1830 and 1880. My critique bears on a different aspect of Rosa Luxemburg's thesis, which has to do with the supposed impossibility of realizing surplus-value in a model of pure capitalism, which I refute through my propositions regarding the active role of credit in the accumulation process.

Things have changed greatly since then. Monopoly capitalism brings with it accelerated generalization of the waged form of labor, so much so that in the United States the crisis of 1930 breaks out in an almost completely wage-earning society. Thence its novel character. And my reading of this first long systemic crisis, then, sees it as the first wave in the decline of capitalism. With generalized monopoly, capitalism completes the process of integration and subordination of the productive system in its entirety. Contemporary capitalism then seeks to overcome its crisis through a new expansion of the field of social activities subordinated to the logic of profit extraction by privatizing public services (the common property) and by inventing a new field of business—the environmental domain, about which I will have more to say.

Marx was right to specify which boundaries of social labor are to be taken into account at each stage of development, and to distinguish between the social labor proper to capitalism and the other forms of labor being carried out in spaces not governed (or not yet governed) by capitalist relations. To call these forms "not socially useful" (for capital) is both true and false. On the one hand, these areas of reality evade direct domination by capital, but on the other, their very existence affects the reproduction conditions of social labor under direct domination of capital.

Feminism made broad contributions to the thought process that allowed full daylight to be thrown onto these "clandestine" relations. For the "free" labor of women in the household framework enables reduction of the real wages paid to those workers selling their labor power. Once again the social space administered by capital cannot be separated from its environment (other social spaces located outside that controlled directly by capital). Once more capitalism's rationality loses its absolute character and becomes relative in the vaster social space surrounding and transcending it. On that vaster scale this rationality even turns into irrationality; for on that scale rationality is inseparable from human emancipation, which involves trespassing beyond mercantile alienation.

Women's labor is not the sole example of these forms working outside the narrow field of capital's direct domination. As soon as one steps outside the restricted field of the capitalist mode of production (the two departments), one is confronted, in the social formations of really existing capitalism, with apparently "independent" forms of labor (like the labor of peasant producers) that in reality are integrated and subordinated (though indirectly) to capital's exploitation, as has already been seen. Inflating Department III with surplus absorption likewise offers new possibilities for expanding the field of operation of capitalist relations. This transformation of capitalism deprives the distinction between productive and unproductive labor of its central place insofar as the waged forms of unproductive labor become a source for the extraction of profits.

Social labor in Marx is always labor operating on the basis of scientific and technical knowledge (every mode of production is "cognitive"; for that reason Marx speaks of a general intellect inseparable from the productivity of social labor), and in a given framework of natural conditions. The problem is, then, to know whether the availability of natural resources is to be viewed as part of the capitalist mode or as located at its boundary.

In this regard, bourgeois economics considers only natural resources fallen into private ownership and thereby having a price. It deals with them as constitutive elements of cost, as factors of production in their own right. So be it. But then it ignores two sets of serious problems: the possible exhaustion of certain resources and the overall effects of their utilization. These are two sets of problems rediscovered by contemporary environmentalism.

Is the "social price" paid through exhaustion a "just" price because it is defined by the supply price of the owners of exhaustible resources? Certainly not, above all when national considerations are reintroduced into the reality of really existing globalized capitalism: the inequality crystallized in the trading of nonrenewable resources for renewable commodities.

Bourgeois economics proposes, to deal with unowned, "free" resources, consideration of the "external economies" involved in access to their utilization. Beyond the difficulties in measuring the former—always mostly artificial—it is hard to see how really existing capitalism might let its functioning be subordinated to their requirements.

Marx does not ignore the problem. He discusses the subject in distinguishing "wealth" from "value." Value is the exclusive product of social labor, socially organized on the basis of capitalist relations. But Marx does not say that wealth is the exclusive product of social labor. He says that the latter is the combined result of the former and of "nature." Private appropriation of certain means of accessing what it offers, especially in regard to the soil, gives under capitalism a "right" to part of the produced value. This is how Marx treats the subject of ground rent. So I am always surprised by the confusions sustained about this by some contemporary Marxists who talk indistinguishably about "wealth" and "value."

On this question I have developed the thesis that capitalism is by its very nature unable to take into account that requirement, which transcends it. But what, then, to put in place of the narrow criteria of capitalist rationality? Knowing that the operation of those criteria strengthens the increasingly destructive side of capitalist accumulation and that, because of this, capitalist economic rationality is social irrationality on the scale of the human race. Marx knew this, said so, but put forward no positive alternative. We know his critique of "utopian socialisms" and his refusal to "give recipes for the cookpots of the future." He leaves to the materialist dialectic the task of settling this future problem, through consciousness and the social class struggle. I share this viewpoint, which does not exclude, but includes, the need to give to critical utopia's fantasies the role that they deserve in building the alternative: twenty-first-century socialism.

Is there any use to our arguments going outside the narrow framework of the capitalist mode? I answer in the affirmative because it is precisely by this means that one can put one's finger on the limits of capitalism's rationality, that one can reveal the conflict pitting its rationality against the higher rationality inseparable from human emancipation. Thus, for example, beyond the concrete political analysis of the composition of the content of the portmanteau represented by Department III, it is necessary to identify those of its elements that though rational from the point of view of capital appreciation are irrational from the point of view of emancipation.

Once again the future, beyond capitalism, is there to build. But it is useful, on this plane as on others, to leave to the creative fantasy of utopia the breathing space allowing it to propose and to act toward building the emancipatory alternative.

The Social Power of Capital

The characteristics of historic capitalism are at the origin of a confusion between the concept of capital and the concrete reality in which it is embodied—producer goods. Bourgeois economics is responsible for this confusion and confesses to it through its claim to discover the specific productivity tied to the utilization of production instruments. Marx is never guilty of this confusion. His concept of capital sees it as a social relationship of production enabling the extraction of surplus value; and the capital that a capitalist must gather to enable this is not limited to the fraction of capital destined for the purchase of production instruments (constant capital) but equally includes that intended for the payment of wages (variable capital).

Social power is a concept that must be handled with great care, for the social power of capital is exercised in a specific way, different from how power was exercised in former societies. With capitalism we are present at a reversal of the ordering of political and economic factors. In the societies that preceded capitalist modernity, the political factor is dominant and the economic subordinate to it. In capitalism, for the first time in history, the economic factor becomes directly dominant. Put crudely, before capitalism power is the source of wealth, in capitalism wealth becomes the source of power. This reversal is at the origin of the emergence of economic science, which claims to discover the laws governing economic life independently from the vicissitudes of politics, in this way dissociating economics from politics.

The forms in which capital exerts its power have, in turn, undergone transformations paralleling the transformation from capitalism into monopoly, and then generalized-monopoly capitalism. In the nineteenth century the power of capital was exercised through the concrete procedures of the epoch's social struggles. This power was in the first place that of the business owners who hire the wage-workers. It must be said: capital employs (and exploits) the workers; it is not the case that the workers simply make use of the means of production. Next, this power is the result of the ability of this new bourgeois class to negotiate a sharing of general (political and economic) power with other social classes—the former aristocracies, the peasantry, or, later and only in part, the working class. The power of the generalized monopolies grows to a new size and exalts itself into a new, exclusive and absolute centralized power. This transformation is accompanied by transformation of the system of prices and incomes that casts aside all reference to values and to surplus-value. The conditions are then brought together so that the immediate reality—the structure of prices and incomes—resulting from society's adjustment to the monopolies' strategies, is alone on stage. One thus has the illusion that capital is no longer anything but the expression of a pure power, that of capital. We have thus reached the deepest level of mercantile alienation, the violence of whose expression is increased yet more by financialization.

The Globalization of Value

The transformation of values into globalized values constitutes a major dimension of the political economy of modern times. Each stage in the development of historic capitalism corresponded to specific forms of this transformation, an analysis of which has been at the center in many of my major works.

That is why I content myself here referring the reader to my book *The Law of Worldwide Value* and to the chapter devoted to the international economy in *Unequal Development*. Marx had aimed to write a chapter of *Capital* devoted to international trade, which never saw daylight. My critique of economic theories about movements in the balance of foreign payments led me to move the discussion to the domain of historical materialism and to conclude that the peripheries were subordinated to unilateral and permanent structural adjustment, shaping their structures in conformity with the requirements of accumulation in the dominant centers.

As far as this synthetic essay is concerned, I will only say that in Marx's epoch the page of the first world system—the mercantilist system—already belongs to the past, although that of the formation of the new imperialist is still to be written. China, the Ottoman Empire, Sub-Saharian Africa generally remain external to the new globalized capitalism a-birthing. Nevertheless, the major British colonial heritage—India— holds a crucial place in it; and it is this domination and not its supposed industrial progress that gave Great Britain its hegemonic position in the nineteenth century.

Struggles and alliances among classes, competition among capitals, and conflicts among powers—realities all pertaining to the domain of historical materialism, and thereby not reducible to economic laws as conventional economics suggests—result in a system that wanders from disequilibrium to disequilibrium without ever tending toward the realization of an equilibrium that could be predefined in economic terms. Capitalism is, by nature, an unstable system. Its characteristic disorder is thus a reality that no economistic reduction can get rid of. But, of course, national regulation is not everything. It is constrained to enlist in the epoch's globalization, itself modeled on conflict among the powers. Once again, the latter is not reducible to some economic competitiveness that could be dissociated from the effects of internal social struggles and of international political and military conflicts.

That whole system of the nineteenth century was thus in movement, and the direction of this movement can be seen: it led to the concentration/centralization of capital. The monopoly capitalism that was to be born from this movement then calls back into question the activity of the ensemble of forces that brought to pass the divergences between the system of values and that of prices and incomes, alike at national levels and at that of globalized capitalism.

Beyond Capitalism: A Look Back at the Concept of Social Value

I have wished, in presenting this synthesis, to take up again the conclusions I had reached in my previous works concerning the analysis of the causes, the directions, and the bearing of the divergences between the system of values and that of prices and incomes such as it was in nineteenth-century competitive capitalism and such as it has become in the contemporary epoch of generalized-monopoly capitalism. This evolution is that of a system that has raised itself above concrete forms of the manifestations of the social power of capital all the way to the final abstract form through which it would express itself henceforward.

The objective of this labor was simply to analyze the reality of contemporary generalized-monopoly capitalism, and, in that way demonstrate that this system is not viable and that its implosion, already ongoing, is inevitable. In this sense contemporary capitalism deserves the adjective "senile" that I have applied to it: the autumn of capitalism. I did not want to go further and put forward political action strategies enabling construction of a positive alternative. To take up that challenge would have required study of fundamental questions that are not touched on, in particular that of active social subjects. Elsewhere I had sketched out the broad outlines of the challenges, which, according to me, cannot be taken up except on condition that bold, radical-leftist movements are recomposed. Then and only then can the autumn of capitalism and the springtime of the peoples coincide. This is not yet the case. The only thing I ascertain is the expected implosion of the system. This is accompanied then by revolts of the southern peoples, the rise of conflicts between the emergent countries and the centers of the historic imperialist Triad, the implosion of the European system, and the rise of new struggles in the centers themselves. All that augurs well for the possibility of radical leftist movements, up to the challenges, being reborn.

The preceding elaborations help answer the question before us: has the progression in the productivity of social labor, arising in the framework of capitalist expansion, brought about "social progress" in a broader, yet to be specified, sense?

The extension of capitalism is ordered by the capitalist law of transformed value, which governs not merely expanded reproduction but, in short, all aspects of social life, which it subordinates to the prioritized requirements of capital appreciation. There is no "market economy," to use the banal fashionable terminology, which does not result in a "market society." The rationality of economic decision making showcased by the bourgeois economists is a relative rationality, that is, irrationality when raised from the level of economic management to that of the entire scope of social life.

The progression of productive forces linked to the unfolding of this logic is not synonymous with unqualified progress. For it has, and always has had, simultaneous constructive and destructive effects. This contradiction, immanent in the materialist dialectic of capitalist extension, worsens to the exact extent that history moves forward in the framework of this system. It has now reached such a point that henceforward the destructive aspects of capitalism can be said to prevail broadly over its progressive contributions. Contemporary environmentalism rightly accentuates this overturn. For my part, I have accentuated a different dimension of the contradiction: the increasing divergence between the material conditions available to majorities in the centers and to those in the peripheries of the global capitalist system, which is the main form of the pauperization that Marx, rightly, linked to the unfolding of the capital/labor contradiction.

Marx's fundamental methodological instrument, the materialist dialectic, had already enabled him to grasp entirely the ambivalence of progress achieved by and within capitalism. Marx says of this mode of production that, with increasing force, it destroys, in step with its expansion, the very foundations of society: "man" (the alienated and exploited workers) and "nature." Thence, Marx concluded, the capitalist system could constitute only one stage in history. The idea that it might be "the end of history" as is said nowadays, or, a bit more elegantly, that it is a system capable of unlimited adaptation to the requirements of change, is scarcely anything but nonsense. Capitalism has adapted, and can still adapt, to many requirements but never those that are essential to the overcoming of its fundamental contradiction. But Marx did not draw from this the conclusion that socialism, defined as a higher, emancipation-based stage in the unfolding of human civilization, was "inevitable." The method of the materialist dialectic forbade that to him. Marx had an open, even though optimistic, vision of the future. He did not exclude "self-destruction," to which he actually referred explicitly. Of course, the Soviet vulgarization that passed for Marxism had declared socialism to be "inevitable." Doing so, it put in place of the materialist dialectic operative in Marx's historical materialism a mechanistic interpretation in which supposed "laws" make up a closed and finished theory of history.

So the question of the future is still open. But we must prepare it, contribute to evolution going toward transcendence of capitalism by building the socialist alternative, and lessen the risks of a self-destructive shipwreck. How are we to prepare that better future based on reason and human emancipation (themselves inseparable)? Marx had put class struggle led by the working class (the proletariat) at the center of his answer to the question. He explicitly said that the coming socialism would be the result of that struggle, and refused to define its content "in advance" too specifically. The method guiding this strategic choice of action—"it is not merely a matter of understanding the world, but of changing it"—is, in my opinion, still valid, on condition that the narrow concept of "working class," tacitly understood as being that of the advanced industrialized countries, be replaced with the much broader totality of lower classes and of dominated and exploited peoples. This would take account of the reality represented by the polarization linked to really existing capitalism's globalized expansion.

Socialism, a stage or series of stages on the long road to communism conceived as a higher phase of human civilization, will certainly have to develop strategies progressively reducing, and finally abolishing, the reign of the capitalist law of transformed value. But what of social value and of the productivity of social labor?

The concept of social value lights our lamp and calls on us to conceive what the construction requirements of the socialism to come are, of an economic management based on the social utility of those goods and services that society in its totality (not the capitalists) decides to produce. It provides us not with a ready-to-be-applied recipe but merely with a principle: fusion between economic and political management and their common subordination to the workings of the egalitarian democracy of all individuals, simultaneously citizens, producers, and consumers, from schoolchildren to pensioners. The consciousness of this necessity is evident: "civilization's discontents" (to pick up Freud's phrase, but giving it a different meaning) are already felt forcibly by all the peoples of the contemporary world.

The propositions for an action strategy to that end, which I have raised in my book *The Implosion of Contemporary Capitalism*, are placed in this perspective of contribution to the rebirth of the radical left, that is to say, radical in its critique of capitalism, whose formulation Marx had begun but in no way completed.

II. THE SURPLUS IN MONOPOLY CAPITALISM AND THE IMPERIALIST RENT

ℂℜ

PAUL BARAN AND PAUL SWEEZY DARED, and were able, to continue the work begun by Marx. Starting from the observation that capitalism's inherent tendency was to allow increases in the value of labor power (wages) only at a rate lower than the rate of increase in the productivity of social labor, they deduced that the disequilibrium resulting from this distortion would lead to stagnation absent systematic organization of ways to absorb the excess profits stemming from that tendency.

This observation was the starting point for the definition they gave to the new concept of "surplus." Baran then extended Marx's analysis of the dynamic of capital accumulation in volume two of *Capital,* restricted to a system reduced to the two Departments of Production of means of production and of consumption goods respectively, with the introduction of a surplus-absorbing Department III.

I have always considered this bold stroke as a crucial contribution to the creative utilization of Marx's thoughts. Baran and Sweezy dared and were able to "start from Marx," but they refused to stop, like so many other Marxists, at the exegesis of his writings.

Having, for my part, completely accepted this crucial contribution from Baran and Sweezy, I would like, in this modest offering devoted to honoring their work, to put forward a "quantitative metric" of that surplus.

Metric of the Surplus

The surplus at issue, then, is the result of growth in the productivity of social labor exceeding the price paid for labor power. Let us assume, for example, that the rate of growth in the productivity of social labor is about 4.5 percent per year, sufficient to double the net product over a period of about fifteen years, corresponding to an assumed average lifetime for capital equipment. Department I consists of investment goods, which equal invested profits, and Department II consists of wage goods, which equal wages. To simplify the argument, we will assume that for both departments the organic compositions of capital and the rates of growth of labor productivity are fixed. To permit changes in those parameters would force us to use algebraic notation for the model, which might easily be done but could make it harder for non-mathematicians to understand. Taking those complications into account would change less than the net product.

So let us assume that, in the long run, real wages would grow at a rate of about 2.5 percent per year to bring about an increase of 40 percent over a fifteen-year span. We end up with changes in the key magnitudes of the model in conformity with the above table (numbers approximated).

At the end of a half-century's regular and continuous evolution of the system, the surplus, which defines the size

Year	Net Revenue	Dept. I	Dept. II	Dept. III
1	100	50	50	0
15	200	70	70	60
30	400	100	100	200
45	800	140	140	520

of Department III relative to net revenue, itself the sum of wages, reinvested profits, and surplus, takes up two-thirds of the net product (roughly equivalent to GDP).[5]

The shift indicated is approximately what happened during the twentieth century in the "developed" centers of world capitalism (the United States/Europe/Japan Triad). Keynes had indeed noted that mature capitalism was stricken by a latent tendency toward persistent stagnation. But he had not explained that tendency, which would have required him to seriously take into account the replacement of the "classical" competitive model by monopoly capitalism. His explanation thus remained tautological: stagnation was the result of the—unexplained—fall in the marginal efficiency of capital or expected profits on new investment (below even the strongest liquidity preference). In contrast, Baran and Sweezy explained to perfection both the tendency toward stagnation and the means used to overcome it. They unraveled the mysteries of contemporary capitalism.

Initially—that is, until the 1914 war—surplus amounted in practice merely to tax-financed state expenditures of at most 10 to 15 percent of GDP. It was a matter of spending to maintain the sovereign (public administration, police, armed forces), of expenditures linked to the public management of some social services (education and public health), and of the installation of some infrastructural elements (roads and bridges, ports, railroad lines). Analysis of the components corresponding to the concept of surplus shows the diversity of the regulations governing their administration.

Corresponding approximately to Marx's Departments I and II in the national accounts are the sectors defined respectively as "primary" (agricultural production and mining), "secondary" (manufacturing), and a portion of so-called tertiary activities that is hard to derive from statistics not designed for that purpose, even when the definition of their status is not itself confusing. To be held to participate—indirectly—in the output of Departments I and II are transportation of implements, raw materials, and finished products; trade in those products; and the cost of managing the financial institutions needed to service the two departments. What are not to be regarded as direct or indirect constitutive elements in their output, and therefore counted as elements of surplus, are government administration, public expenditures and transfer payments (for education, health, social security, pensions, and old-age benefits), services (advertising) corresponding to selling costs, and personal services paid for from income (including housing).

Whether the "services" at issue, lumped together in the national accounts under the title "tertiary activities" (with the possibility of distinguishing among them a new sector termed quaternary), are administered by public or private entities does not by itself qualify them as belonging to Department III (the surplus). The fact remains that the volume of "tertiary" activities in the developed countries of the center (and also in many of the peripheral countries, though that question—a different one—does not concern us here) is much larger than that of the primary and secondary sector. Moreover, the sum of taxes and obligatory contributions in those countries by itself amounts to or exceeds 40 percent of their GDP. Talk by some fundamentalist right-wing ideologists calling for "reduction" of these fiscal extractions is purely demagogic: capitalism can no longer function in any other way. In reality, any possible decrease in the taxes paid by the "rich" must necessarily be made up by heavier taxation on the "poor."

We can thus estimate without risk of major error that the "surplus" (Department III) accounts for half of GDP or, in other terms, has grown from 10 percent of GDP in the nineteenth century to 50 percent in the first decade of the twenty-first century. So if—in Marx's day—an analysis of accumulation limited to consideration of Departments I and II made sense, this is no longer the case. The enrichment of Marxist thought by Baran, Sweezy, and Harry Magdoff (long-time editor with Sweezy of *Monthly Review*) through their taking account of Department III (and the linked concept of surplus, defined as we have recalled it) is for that reason decisive. I find it deplorable that this is still doubted by a majority of the analysts of contemporary Marxism!

Once again, not everything in this surplus is to be condemned as useless or parasitical. Far from it! On the contrary, growth in a large fraction of the expenditures linked to Department III is worthy of support. For a more advanced stage in the unfolding of human civilization, spending on such activities as education, health care, social security, and retirement—or even other socializing "services" linked to democratic forms of structuring alternatives to structuring by the market, such as public transport, housing, and others—would be summoned to take on even more importance. In contrast, some constitutive elements of Department III—like the "selling costs" that grew so fabulously during the twentieth century—are evidently of a parasitic nature and were viewed early on as such by some economists, like Joan Robinson, who were minimized or disparaged by their profession. Some public (weapons) and some private (security guards, legal departments) expenditures likewise are parasitic. A fraction of Department III, to be sure, is (or should we say was?) made up of spending that benefits workers and complements their wages (health care and unemployment insurance, pensions). Just the same, these benefits, won by the working classes through intense struggle, have been called into question during the past three decades, some have been cut back severely, others have shifted from provision by a public authority based on the principle of social solidarity to private management supposedly "freely bargained for" on the basis of "individual rights." This management technique, prevalent in the United States and expanding in Europe, opens supplementary, and very lucrative, areas for the investment of surplus.

The fact remains that in capitalism all these usages of the GDP—whether "useful" or not—fulfill the same function: to allow accumulation to continue despite the growing insufficiency of labor incomes. What is more, the permanent battle over transferring many fundamental elements of Department III from public to private management opens supplemental opportunities for capital to "make a profit" (and thereby increase the volume of surplus!). Private medical care tells us that "If the sick are to be treated it must above all be profitable"—to private clinics, to laboratories, to pharmaceutical manufacturers, and to the insurers! My analysis of Department III of surplus absorption stands within the spirit of the pioneering work of Baran and Sweezy. The necessary conclusion is that a large proportion of the activities managed on those terms are parasitic and inflate the GDP, thus reducing drastically its significance as an indicator of the real "wealth" of a society.

Counterposed to this is the current fashion of considering the rapid growth of Department III as a sign of the transformation of capitalism, its passage from the "industrial age" into a new stage, the "knowledge economy." Capital's unending pursuit of realization would thus regain its legitimacy. The expression "knowledge capitalism" is itself an oxymoron. Tomorrow's economy, the socialist economy, would indeed be a "knowledge economy": capitalism can never be such. To fantasize that the development of the productive forces by itself is establishing—within capitalism—tomorrow's economy, as the writings of Antonio Negri and his students would have us believe, has only a seeming validity. In reality, the realization of capital, necessarily based on the oppression of labor, wipes out the progressive aspect of this development. This annihilation is at the core of the development of Department III, designed to absorb the surplus inseparable from monopoly capitalism.

We must therefore avoid confounding today's reality (capitalism) with a fantasy about the future (socialism). Socialism is not a more adequate form of capitalism, doing the same things but only better and with a fairer income distribution. Its governing paradigm—socialization of management over direct production of use values—thus comports exactly with a powerful development of some of the expenditures which currently, under capitalism, take part in its main function, surplus absorption.

Order of Magnitude of the Imperialist Rent

In its globalized setup, capitalism is inseparable from imperialist exploitation of its dominated peripheries by its dominant centers. Under monopoly capitalism that exploitation takes the form of monopoly rents—in ordinary language, the superprofits of multinational corporations—that are themselves by and large imperialist rents.

In the propositions that I have put forward formulating the terms of a globalized law of value I stated the full importance of this rent.[6] Here I would like to give an idea of its quantitative scope in the capitalism of generalized monopolies and to link its effects to those associated with surplus absorption.

The order of magnitude of the quantifiable fraction of the imperialist rent, the result of the differential in the prices of labor powers of equal productivity, is obviously large. In order to give a sense of that order of magnitude, we hypothesize a division of the world's gross product in the ratio of two-thirds for the centers (20 percent of the world's population) and one-third for the peripheries (80 percent of the population). We assume an annual rate of growth of gross product of 4.5 percent for both centers and peripheries, and a rate of growth of wages of 3.5 percent for the centers but total stagnation (zero growth) for peripheral wages. After fifteen years of development in this model we would arrive at the results summarized in the above table.

Of course, the volume of this imperialist rent, which seems to be on the order of half the Gross Domestic Product of the peripheries, or 17 percent of the world's Gross Product and 25 percent of the centers' GDPs, is partially hidden by exchange rates. It is a question here of a well-known reality that introduces uncertainty into international comparisons:

Year		Centers	Peripheries	World
1	Gross Product	66	33	100
	Wages	33	17	50
	Profits	33	16	50
45	Gross Product	132	68	200
	Wages	56	17	73
	Profits	56	17	73
	Department III	20	—	20
	Imperialist Rent	—	34	34

Are GDP value comparisons to be made in terms of market exchange rates or according to exchange rates reflecting purchasing-power parities? Moreover, the rent is not transferred as a net benefit to the centers (United States, Europe, Japan). That the local ruling classes hold on to some of it is itself the condition for their agreement to "play the globalization game." But the fact remains that the material benefits drawn from this rent, accruing not only to the profit of capital ruling on a world scale but equally to the profit of the centers' opulent societies, are more than considerable.[7]

In addition to the quantifiable advantages linked to differential pricing of labor powers, there are others, non-quantifiable but no less crucial, based on exclusive access to the planet's material resources, on technological monopolies, and on control over the globalized financial system.

The share of imperialist rent transferred from the peripheries to the centers accentuates in its turn the global disequilibrium pointed out by Baran and forms an additional factor, swelling the surplus to be absorbed. The contrast to be observed during the present phase of the crisis, between weak growth in the centers and rapid growth in the developing countries of the periphery, is to be understood only in terms of an overall analysis linking analysis of how surplus is absorbed to analysis of the extraction of imperialist rent.

III. Abstract Labor and the Wage-Scale

☙

THE CONCEPT OF ABSTRACT LABOR, formulated by Marx, defines the common denominator allowing summation of different forms of simple (unskilled) and complex (skilled) labor. We are dealing with a concept central to the theory of value.

Simple Labor, Complex Labor, Abstract Labor

The unit of abstract labor, whether an hour or a year of abstract social labor, is a composite unit combining units of simple (unskilled) and complex (skilled) labor in some given proportion.

The concept of abstract labor is central to Marx's elaboration of the law of value, that is, to the determination of a commodity's value by the quantity of labor required to produce it and to the division of that value between wages and surplus value. The concepts of simple (unskilled) and complex (requiring training) labor are easily understood. But that of abstract labor is not immediately visible because a society's products do not stem from workers separated one from the other but from a collectivity, abstracted from which neither the least-skilled nor the most-skilled labor has any meaning: production requires their joint contribution.

We place the ensuing reflections in the context of a complete and closed capitalist system, which presents the three following characteristics: (1) the only form of commodity-producing labor is that which is supplied by wage workers who sell their labor power to capital; (2) the system by itself accounts for production of all consumer goods and producer goods in the proportions necessary to assure its simple or expanded reproduction; (3) there is no foreign trade.

Let us choose, from this society, a sample of one hundred workers distributed among the different categories of (differently skilled) workers in exactly similar proportions to their distribution in the overall society (whose labor force, for example, might number 30 million).

In the following simplified analysis we take account of only two categories of labor: (1) simple labor involves only 60 percent of the sample (sixty workers); (2) complex labor involves 40 percent of the sample (forty workers).

We assume that each year the workers in the sample provide the same annual number of labor hours, say, 8 hours per day and 220 days per year. So each of them provides, each year, a labor year amounting to 1,760 labor hours. Later we will calculate the quantity of labor years. So in each year a simple (unskilled) worker contributes one year of simple labor to the collective social labor, while a skilled worker provides a contribution to one year of complex labor. We abstract from the cost of training simple workers because this training is that which is provided to all citizens. Contrariwise, we take into consideration the cost of supplementary training for skilled workers. The latter, for example, would extend for ten years and for each of those years would cost, for each worker involved, the equivalent of two years of social labor to cover the cost of teachers, training equipment, and the student's living expenses.

Whereas the unskilled worker would work for thirty years, the skilled one would work for only twenty years, having devoted the first ten years to being trained. The cost of this training (twenty years of social labor) would be recovered over twenty years of this labor through the valorization of complex labor. In other words, the unit of complex labor (an hour or a year) would be worth two units of simple labor.

It follows that 60 percent of a composite unit of abstract labor would consist of the equivalent of one unit of simple labor, and 40 percent of the equivalent of one unit of complex labor (worth two units of simple labor). In other words, one unit of abstract labor provided by the labor collective is worth 1.4 units of simple labor.

I call attention to the following remarks:

1. The value of a commodity is to be measured according to the quantity of abstract labor required for its production because none of the workers works in isolation; he is nothing apart from the team in which he or she is a part. Production is collective and the productivity labor is that of the social labor collective, not that of team members taken separately one from the other.

2. I have put forth an extreme hypothesis in regard to the average cost of training for skilled workers. In the real world such training takes only a few weeks of apprenticeship for some, one or two years for others, and longer only for a few of the most highly skilled. A calculation comprising a dozen categories, allocated correctly according to their relative numbers, the time and costs of their training, and their labor time over the course of their entire lives would certainly reveal a value for an hour of abstract labor lower than 1.4 hours of simple labor. Abstract labor

is not a "multiple" of simple labor; it is larger by a mere fraction.

3. I have accounted for the cost of training and its repayment without mention of any "discounting of the future," and so without assigning a "price" to time to take account of the fact that training time takes place before those costs are recuperated through the valorization of skilled labor. I have proceeded in this manner because the generations being trained, presently at work and in retreat, make up, all together, society as it exists at any given moment.

4. I have developed a line of argument based on the initial approximation. Training costs are to be measured in years of abstract labor (collective social labor), not in years of simple labor. One might develop a second corrective approximation. Or better yet, formulate a mathematical model that would introduce into the formulation of the interdependence of magnitudes the conversion of simple labor into abstract labor. Its results would not much differ qualitatively from those provided by my initial approximation.

5. I have not introduced into my argument the scale of real wages received by each category of workers, only the cost of their training, which is the sole "price" paid by the society to dispose of the labor force appropriate to its productions.

Production of Surplus Value, Consumption of Surplus Value

The value of the team's annual production and the measure of the extraction of a surplus value on this occasion are to be calculated in quantities of abstract labor.

	Contributions to the Formation of Value (Labor Years)			Contributions to the Formation of Surplus Value (Labor Years)	
	Hourly Labor	Abstract Labor		Wages	Surplus Value
Simple Workers	60	60	60	30	30
Complex Workers	40	40	80	40	40
Total	**100**	**100**	**140**	70	70

Under hypothesis 1, and for our team of 100 workers, we assume that the real wage given to each skilled worker is double that of a simple worker, this relationship being that of the value of an hour of complex labor to that of an hour of simple labor. We have the above table.

It is easy to recognize that the wage for a skilled worker is double that for an unskilled worker, as the former contributes twice as much to the value of the product as does the latter. Both equally contribute to the extraction of surplus value, in the same proportion. The rate of surplus value here is 100 percent. For an hour of labor provided by a simple worker, he receives a wage allowing him to buy consumption goods whose value is equal to one half hour of abstract labor. Each labor hour provided by a skilled worker is worth twice as much and likewise his wage is twice as large, allowing him to buy consumption goods whose value is equal to one hour of abstract labor.

We now take a wage scale different from that which would imply a equality between the wage and the contribution to the formation of value. In this second hypothesis the wage retained by a skilled worker is four times (rather than double) that of a simple worker.

	Contributions to the Formation of Value (Labor Years)			Contributions to the Formation of Surplus Value (Labor Years)	
	Hourly Labor	Abstract Labor		Wages	Surplus Value
Simple Workers	60	60	60	30	30
Complex Workers	40	40	80	80	0
Total	**100**	**100**	**140**	**110**	**30**

We would then have the table above. Under this hypothesis we recognize that only unskilled workers contribute to the formation of surplus value; the skilled workers "devour" the surplus value to whose formation they contribute.

It then is quite clear that if the wage scale for the various categories of skilled labor has a broad extent, going, say, from 1.5 to 2 times the subsistence minimum (the wage for unskilled labor) for many, three to four times as much for some, and much more for a tiny (extra-skilled) minority, we would recognize that if the majority of workers contribute to the formation of surplus value, although in different proportions (and this gives its full meaning to the term "super-exploited" for the majority—two-thirds—of the workers), there exists a category of the supposed "extra-skilled" (who may sometimes actually be so) who consume more surplus value than what they contribute to its formation.

Some Concluding Reflections

Marx's criticism of the classic bourgeois political economy of Smith and Ricardo concluded by a necessary shifting from analysis centered on "the market" (waves visible on the surface of the sea) to one centered on the depths of production where value and the extraction of surplus value are determined. Without this shifting of analysis from the superficial to the essential, from the apparent to the concealed, no radical critique of capitalism is possible.

In Marx's analysis there exists only one "productivity," that of social labor defined by "the quantities" of abstract labor contained in the commodity produced by a collective of workers.

There is improvement in the productivity of social labor when to produce a unit with a defined use value society can devote a lesser quantity of total abstract labor (direct and indirect). This improvement is produced by progress in the technologies put to work on the basis of society's scientific knowledge. One can compare the productivities of social labor in two production units making the same use values; contrariwise it is meaningless to compare the productivities of social labor in two branches of production making different use values. Thus to compare the general productivity of social labor in two successive epochs of capitalist development (or, more broadly, historical epochs), like productivity comparisons between two systems (for example, two countries), involves reasoning by analogy. The measure of this general productivity is obtained by calculating the weighted average of productivity progress in the different branches producing analogous use values. This is an approximate calculation, the number of use values needing to be considered far exceeding that available for consideration, and the weighting itself being partially dependent on the evolution of productivity in each of the branches under consideration.

The law of value formulated by Marx, based on the concept of abstract labor, expresses the rationality of the social utility (the utility for society) of a defined use value. This rationality transcends that which governs the reproduction of a particular mode of production (in this case, the capitalist mode of production). Under capitalism rationality demands the accumulation of capital, itself based on the extraction of surplus value. The price system frames the operation of this rationality. Economic decisions in this framework of given prices and incomes—themselves defined by the proportion in which value, termed value-added, is shared between wages and profits—will be different from those that might be made on the basis of the law of value that would define, in the socialism to come, the mode of social governance over economic decision making.

Bourgeois economic theory attempts to prove that the mode of decision making in the framework of its system of prices and incomes produces a rational allocation of labor and capital resources synonymous with an optimum pattern of output. But it can reach that goal only through cascading tautological arguments. To do so it artificially slices productivity into "components" attributed to "factors of production."

Although this pattern of slices has no scientific value and rests only on tautological argument, it is "useful" because it is the only way to legitimize capital's profits. The operative method of this bourgeois economics to determine "the wage" by the marginal productivity of "the last employee hired" stems from the same tautology and breaks up the unity of the collective, the sole creator of value. Moreover, contrary to the unproven affirmations of conventional economics, employers do not make decisions by using such "marginal calculation."

The wage scale under real capitalism is not determined by the cost of training skilled workers. It is broadly larger and has no other explanation except through considering the history of concrete social formations and class struggles. Its attempted legitimization through the "marginal productivities" of the contributions of different categories of workers is tautological.

The fundamental inequality in capitalism's characteristic distribution of income rests primarily on the contrast opposing the power of capital owners to the submission of labor power sellers. The wage scale comes as an addition to that. But the latter has by now acquired a new dimension. The contemporary capitalist system of generalized monopolies is based on an extreme centralization of control over capital, accompanied by a generalization of wage labor. In these conditions a large fraction of profit is disguised in the form of the "wages" (or quasi-wages) of the higher layers of the "middle classes" whose activities are those of the servants of capital. The separation among the formation of value, the extraction of surplus value, and its distribution has become wider.

References and Complementary Readings

This text makes up, with two articles published in *Monthly Review*: "Surplus in Monopoly Capital," *Monthly Review* 64/3 (July–August 2012); and "Abstract Labor," forthcoming), a trilogy that I hope will be read as a totality. The theses put forward in this abbreviated text were occasion for argued elaborations in the following of my works:

1. *The Law of Worldwide Value* (New York: Monthly Review Press, 2010)

- The unavoidable detour by way of value, transformation, divergence between profit rates expressed in prices and in values, the failure of equilibrium theories (Walras and Sraffa), price structure, and income distribution, are inseparable in the capitalist law of value (pp. 30–44).
- Chapter on rent: economic law or historical materialism? (pp. 77–81).
- Chapter on interest: State and money cannot be dissociated (pp. 64–70).

2. *Unequal Development* (New York: Monthly Review Press, 1976)

- Chapter on money and credit: the active role of credit in accumulation (critique of Rosa Luxemburg) (pp. 84–88).
- Chapter on money and credit: from the gold standard to floating exchange rates; national policies of regulating accumulation through credit (pp. 88–92).

3. *From Capitalism to Civilization* (Delhi: Tulika Books, 2010)

- The concept of the productivity of social labor; critique of the conventional theory of the productivity of factors of production (pp. 57–67).

The text barely sketches out the major question of globalization and the transformation of value into globalized value, a question constituting the prime object of many of my writings, the most recent formulation, *The*

Law of Worldwide Value. Also to be considered: John Smith, "Imperialism and the Law of Value" (Ph.D. diss., University of Sheffield, UK, 2010). Our two studies, carried out unknown to each other, yielded similar conclusions about the origin of the contemporary imperialist rent. He likewise merely sketches two major subjects, financialization and ecology, for which I refer the reader to the following writings of John Bellamy Foster: *The Ecological Revolution* (New York: Monthly Review Press, 2009); and, with Fred Magdoff, *The Great Financial Crisis* (New York: Monthly Review Press, 2009).

Also see Samir Amin, "Capitalism and the Ecological Footprint," *Monthly Review* 61/6 (November 2009); and "Unequal Access to the Planet's Resources" and "The Extractive Rent" in *The Law of Worldwide Value*, pp. 95–100.

Concerning the nature of Marx's project, I refer the reader to Michael Löwy's excellent *Les aventures de Karl Marx contre le baron de Munchhausen* (Paris: Syllepse, 2012).

Concerning my rapid allusions to Marx's anthropology, see Yvon Quiniou, *L'homme selon Marx* (Paris: Kimé, 2011); and Anton Pannekoek and Patrick Tort, *Darwinisme et Marxisme* (Paris: Arkhé, 2011).

Concerning the subject of the power of capital, see Jonathan Nitzan and Shimshon Bichler, *Capital as Power: A Study of Order and Creorder* (New York: Routledge, 2009).

On the natural complement to this trilogy about the vision of long-run capitalism, see these works of mine:

* *Ending the Crisis of Capitalism or Ending Capitalism?* (Oxford: Pambazuka Books, 2011), esp. "Capitalism, a Parenthesis in History," pp. 56–59.
* *Unequal Development* (New York: Monthly Review Press, 1976), esp. "The Theory of the Balance of Payments," pp. 104–32. In this book, see my critiques of economic theories on international trade, of capital flows, and of fluctuations in the balance of payments. International political economy, which has certainly made a great contribution to correcting conventional economic theory, remains nevertheless limited by the positivist leaning of its methodology.

- Samir Amin and André Gunder Frank, "Let's Not Wait for 1984," in Samir Amin and André Gunder Frank, *Reflections on the World Economic Crisis* (New York: Monthly Review Press, 1978).
- "Market Economy or Oligopoly Capital?" *Monthly Review* 59/11 (April 2008).
- "Historical Capitalism in Decline," *Monthly Review* 62/2 (June 2011).
- *Beyond US Hegemony* (London: Zed, 2006), esp. "The New Imperialism of the Triad," chap. 1.
- *Obsolescent Capitalism* (London: Zed, 2003), esp. "The Political Economy of the 20th Century," pp. 7–17, and "The New Triad Imperialism," pp. 57–72.
- *Global History: A View from the South* (Oxford: Pambazuka Books, 2011), esp. "The Challenge of Globalization," pp. 67ff.

See also Isaac Johsua, *La crise de 1929 et l'émergence américaine* (Paris: PUF, 1999). Johsua calls attention to the new character of this crisis, which functions in an almost entirely waged society.

The analysis of the ongoing implosion of the globalized system of generalized monopolies and the discussion about the conditions for a socialist alternative do not make up the subject of this book, but see *The Implosion of Contemporary Capitalism* (New York: Monthy Review Press, 2013).

In this essay, I have not referred to the innumerable writings of Marxists who read Marx differently than I do. But I refer the reader to the writings of Suzanne de Brunhoff about Marx's monetary theory, according to which demand for money creates its supply. See S. de Brunhoff, *L'Offre de monnaie* (Paris: PUF, 1971). I believe that I have provided an indispensable complement to those writings by proving that the demand for money can be computed. I likewise refer the reader to the book by Nitzan and Bichler cited above. The latter part illustrates perfectly my thesis on "abstract" contemporary capitalism and its financialization. On the other hand, the preceding discussions in this book seem to me to stem from a positive reading that ignores the nature of Marx's project.

Notes

1. S. Amin and A. G. Frank, "Let's Not Wait for 1984," in *Reflections on the World Economic Crisis*, ed. S. Amin and A. G. Frank (New York: Monthly Review Press, 1978).

2. Samir Amin, *Empire of Chaos* (New York: Monthly Review Press, 1992).

3. Samir Amin, *The Implosion of Contemporary Capitalism* (New York: Monthly Review Press, 2013).

4. Samir Amin, *Unequal Development: An Essay on the Social Formations of Peripheral Capitalism* (New York: Monthly Review Press, 1976).

5. In this numerical example we assume that prices are proportional to labor values; that is, the organic composition of capital is the same throughout the economy and rates of exploitation (wages divided by profits) are also equal. If markets were competitive, then, as per standard neoclassical economic theory, wages would rise by the same percentage as the rise in labor productivity. In this example, wages would rise by 4.5 percent, the same as the increase we assume in productivity. However, under monopoly capital conditions, wages rise by less than productivity (abstracting from labor struggle that might force wages up). This means that over time the gap between the total output of a society and wages gets larger and larger. This is represented by the surplus in the last column of the example. This surplus has to be absorbed somewhere in the economy to avoid stagnation.

6. Samir Amin, *The Law of Worldwide Value* (New York: Monthly Review Press, 2010).

7. In this numerical example, we extend the analysis of the surplus to the global economy. Here monopoly capital is able to move around the globe and use its economic and political power to pay workers in the periphery of global capitalism a wage considerably below that in the centers, even though their productivities are the same. For clarity of exposition, we assume that wages in the peripheral countries do not increase at all. This results in an enormous growth of surplus in the periphery, much of which is siphoned

off as imperial rent and ends up in the centers via multinational corporations. The super-profits (based upon superexploitation of the wage labor) then have to be absorbed, making the stagnation tendency analyzed by Baran and Sweezy potentially more difficult to overcome.